W9-CER-655

Prehistoric Animals

DUCK-BILLED DINOSAURS

WINDMILL BOOKS™

New York

Published in 2016 by **Windmill Books**,
an Imprint of Rosen Publishing
29 East 21st Street, New York, NY 10010

Designed and illustrated *by* David West

Cataloging-in-Publication Data
West, David.
Duck-billed dinosaurs / by David West.
p. cm. — (Prehistoric animals)
Includes index.
ISBN 978-1-5081-9018-9 (pbk.)
ISBN 978-1-5081-9019-6 (6-pack)
ISBN 978-1-5081-9020-2 (library binding)
1. Hadrosauridae — Juvenile literature. 2. Dinosaurs — Juvenile literature.
I. West, David, 1956-. II. Title.
QE862.O65 W47 2016
567.914—d23

Manufactured in the United States of America

CPSIA Compliance Information: Batch #BW16PK: For Further Information contact Rosen Publishing, New York, New York at 1-800-237-9932

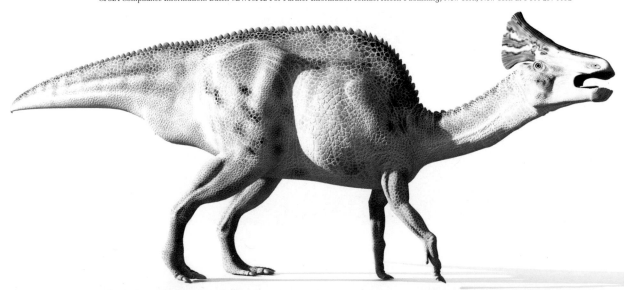

Contents

Corythosaurus means "Helmet Lizard."

Corythosaurus grew up to 35 feet (10.7 m) in length and weighed 4 tons (3.6 metric tons).

Corythosaurus's crest contained air passages that were connected to its nose and lungs.

Corythosaurus

ko-RITH-uh-SAWR-us

This duck-billed dinosaur had a helmet-shaped crest on its head. Scientists think the crest was used to make the dinosaur's sounds louder. It may have made sounds similar to those of a musical wind instrument.

Edmontosaurus

ed-MON-tuh-SAWR-us

Edmontosaurus, like most duckbills, probably walked on all fours some of the time. When it was chased by **predators** it would run away very quickly on its two back legs.

Edmontosaurus grew up to 42 feet (13 m) in length and weighed 3.8 tons (3.4 metric tons).

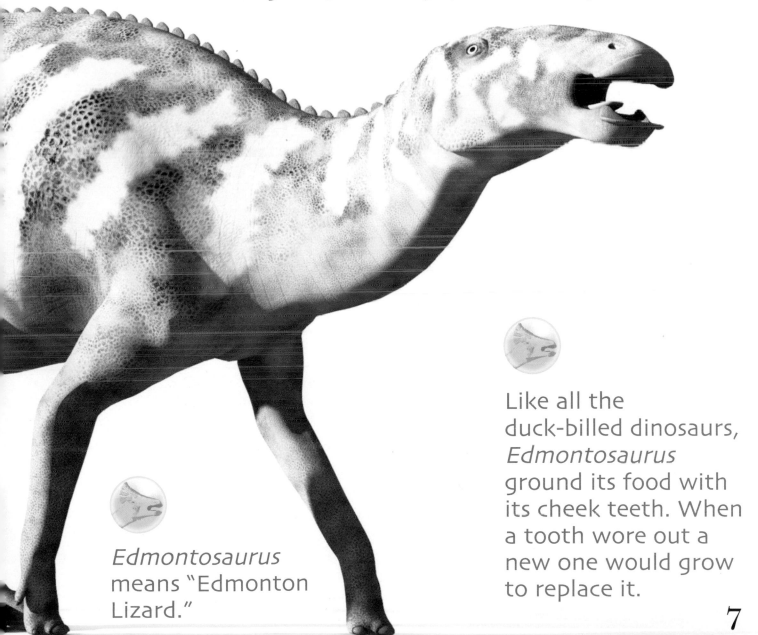

Like all the duck-billed dinosaurs, *Edmontosaurus* ground its food with its cheek teeth. When a tooth wore out a new one would grow to replace it.

Edmontosaurus means "Edmonton Lizard."

7

Lambeosaurus

LAM-be-uh-SAWR-us

Lambeosaurus is one of the few dinosaurs whose fossils show soft skin, so we know that its skin had a thick,

rough, and pebbly texture.

Lambeosaurus grew up to 40 feet (12.2 m) in length and weighed 4–6 tons (3.6–5.4 metric tons).

Lambeosaurus means "Lambe's Lizard" after Lawrence Lambe, an early Canadian **paleontologist**.

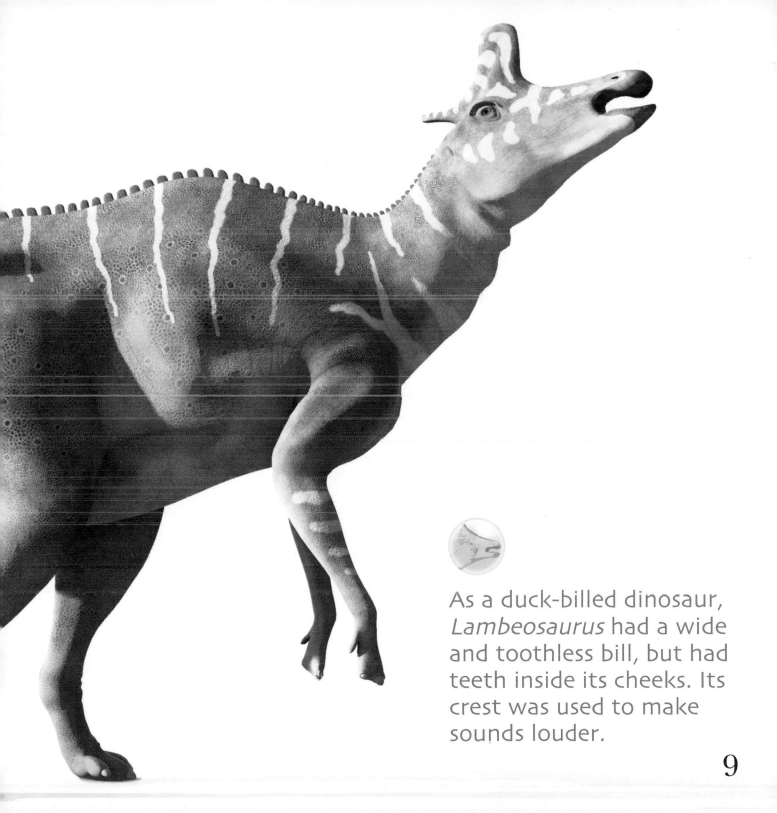

As a duck-billed dinosaur, *Lambeosaurus* had a wide and toothless bill, but had teeth inside its cheeks. Its crest was used to make sounds louder.

9

Lurdusaurus

LAWR-duh-SAWR-us

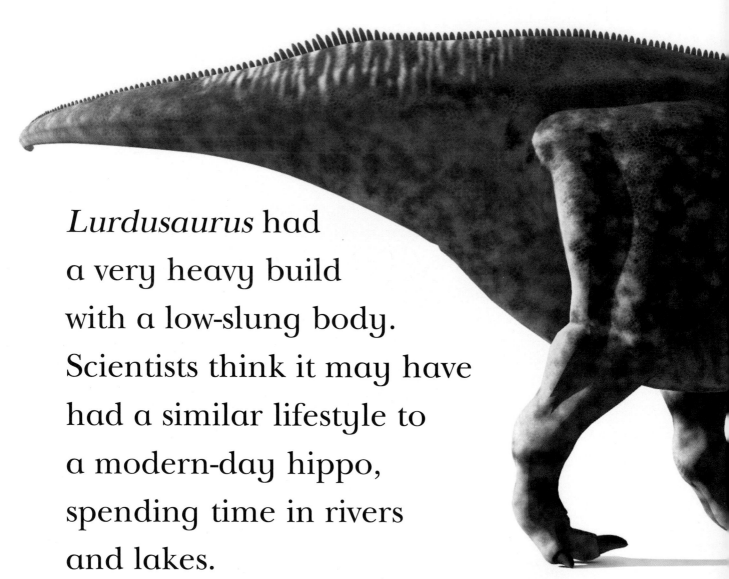

Lurdusaurus had a very heavy build with a low-slung body. Scientists think it may have had a similar lifestyle to a modern-day hippo, spending time in rivers and lakes.

Lurdusaurus means "Heavy Lizard."

 Lurdusaurus grew up to 30 feet (9.1 m) in length and weighed 6 tons (5.4 metric tons).

Lurdusaurus's thumb claws would have made dangerous weapons, able to inflict serious damage on a predator.

Maiasaura means "Good Mother Lizard."

Maiasaura grew up to 30 feet (9.1 m) in length and weighed 4 tons (3.6 metric tons).

Herds of *Maiasaura* built nesting **colonies** that were packed closely together, like those of seabird colonies today.

Maiasaura

mah-ee-ah-SAWR-uh

This large duck-billed dinosaur had a very caring nature. Parents looked after their young once they had hatched from their eggs. A nest could have up to 40 eggs in it.

Olorotitan

oh-LOW-rhu-tye-tan

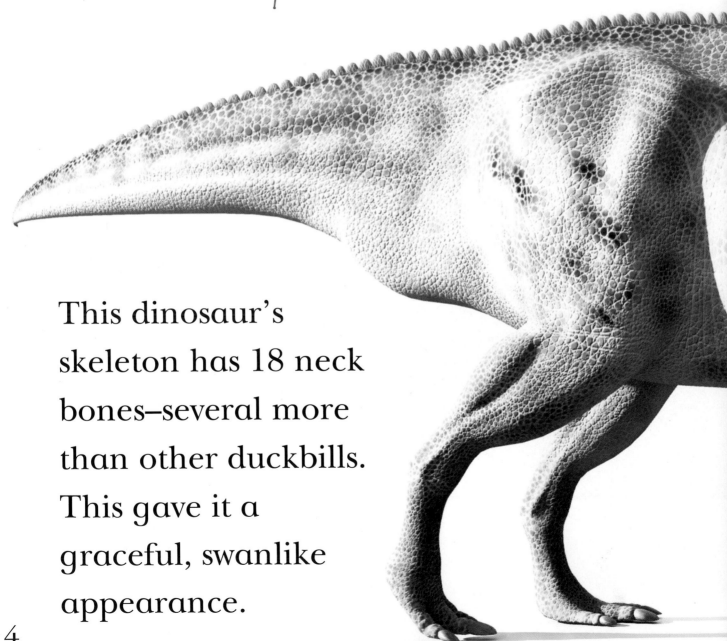

This dinosaur's skeleton has 18 neck bones–several more than other duckbills. This gave it a graceful, swanlike appearance.

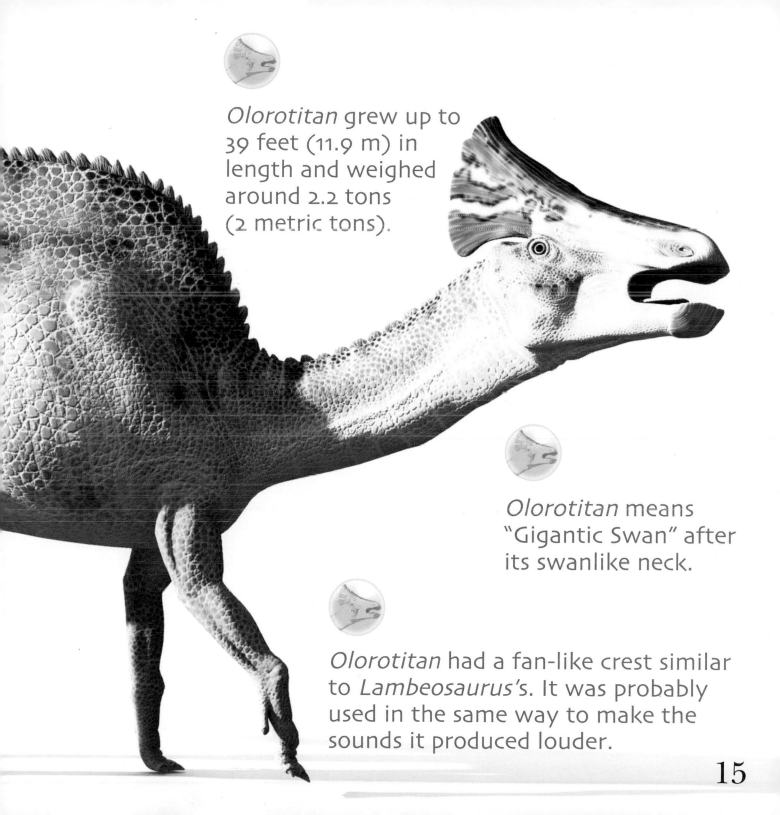

Olorotitan grew up to 39 feet (11.9 m) in length and weighed around 2.2 tons (2 metric tons).

Olorotitan means "Gigantic Swan" after its swanlike neck.

Olorotitan had a fan-like crest similar to *Lambeosaurus's*. It was probably used in the same way to make the sounds it produced louder.

Parasaurolophus

par-ah-SAWR-OL-uh-fus

With its long, distinctive, backward-curving crest, *Parasaurolophus* is one of the most recognizable duck-billed dinosaurs.

Paleontologists made a computer model of its crest, based on fossils, and fed it with a virtual blast of air. The crest produced a deep, reedy sound.

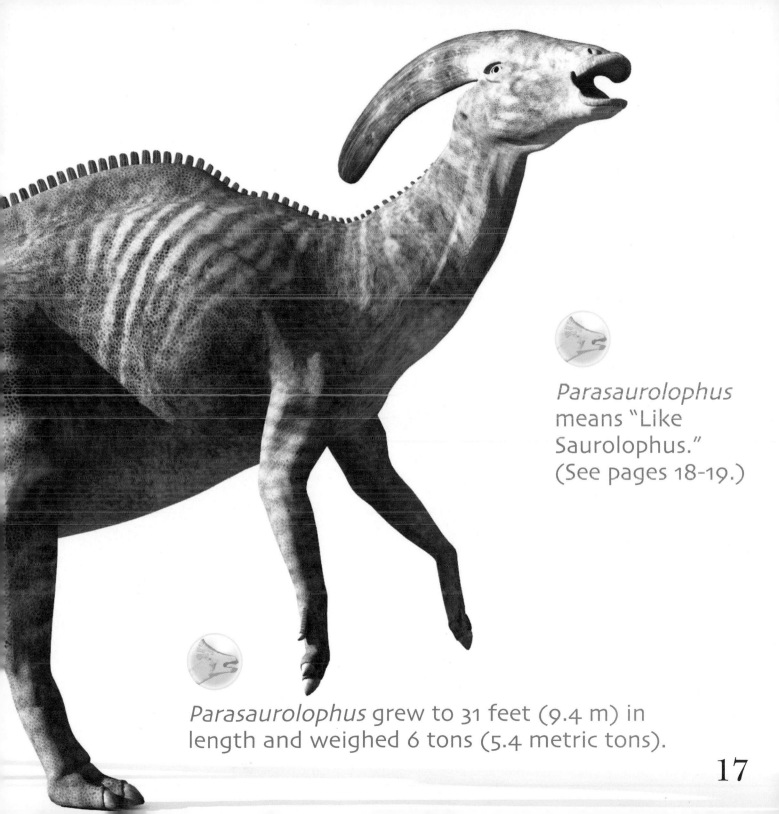

Parasaurolophus
means "Like
Saurolophus."
(See pages 18-19.)

Parasaurolophus grew to 31 feet (9.4 m) in
length and weighed 6 tons (5.4 metric tons).

17

Saurolophus means "Crested Lizard."

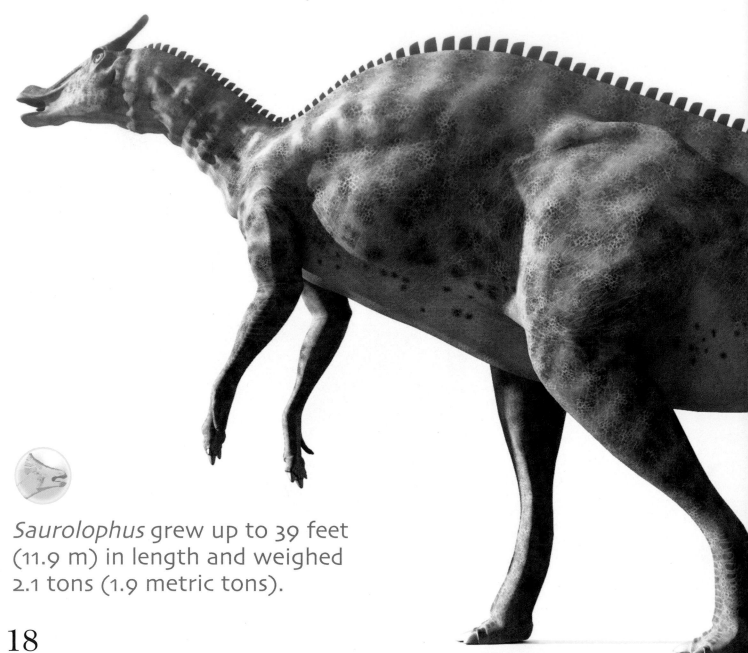

Saurolophus grew up to 39 feet
(11.9 m) in length and weighed
2.1 tons (1.9 metric tons).

Saurolophus

SAWR-OL-o-fus

Saurolophus, like all duckbills, used its tough beak to bite off conifer needles, twigs, seeds, and **cycads.** It then ground them with its back teeth.

Duckbills like *Saurolophus* might have used their crests to sound warning signals about a predator to the rest of their herd.

19

Shantungosaurus means "Shantung Lizard."

Shantungosaurus was 50 feet (15.2 m) in length and 15 tons (13.6 metric tons) in weight.

Many fossils of this dinosaur have been found together, suggesting that they lived in herds.

20

Shantungosaurus

shan-TUNG-o-SAWR-us

Shantungosaurus was the biggest duck-billed dinosaur that ever lived. Like many other hadrosaurs, *Shantungosaurus* had a very long, tapering tail. It used this to balance itself as it ran on its two back legs.

21

Shuangmiaosaurus

San-mi-SAWR-us

Fossil remains of *Shuangmiaosaurus* were found in China quite recently. Although it is considered to be a duck-billed dinosaur some scientists think it may be more closely related to *Iguanodon*.

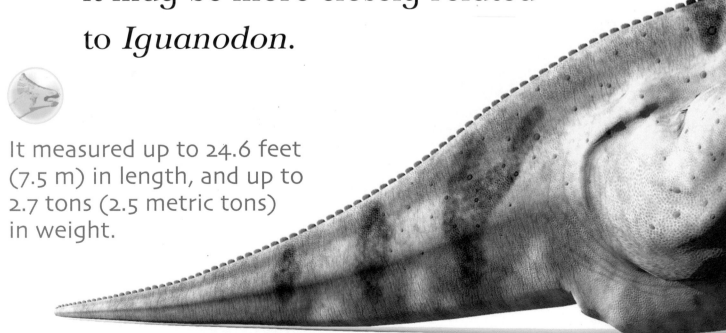

It measured up to 24.6 feet (7.5 m) in length, and up to 2.7 tons (2.5 metric tons) in weight.

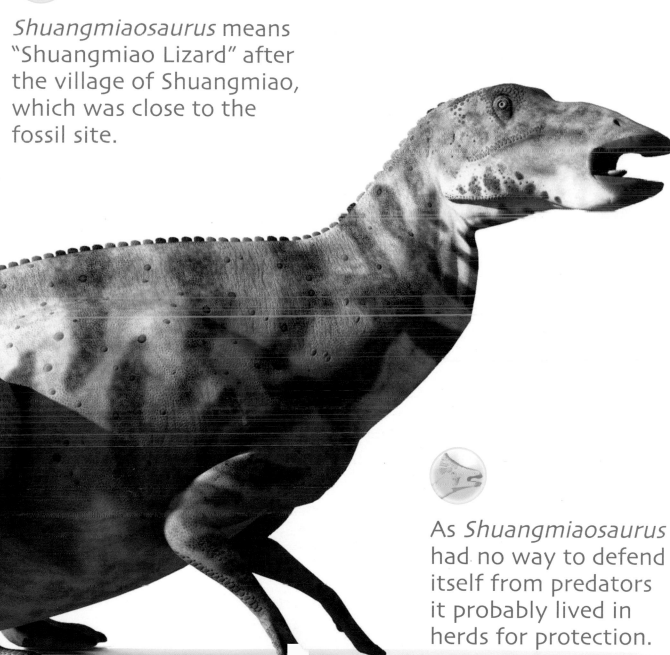

 Shuangmiaosaurus means "Shuangmiao Lizard" after the village of Shuangmiao, which was close to the fossil site.

As *Shuangmiaosaurus* had no way to defend itself from predators it probably lived in herds for protection.

Glossary

colonies
Groups of animals living close together.

cycads
Palmlike plants.

paleontologist
A scientist who studies early forms of life, chiefly by examining fossils.

predators
Animals that hunt and kill other animals for food.

Timeline

Dinosaurs lived during the Mesozoic Era, which is divided into three main periods.

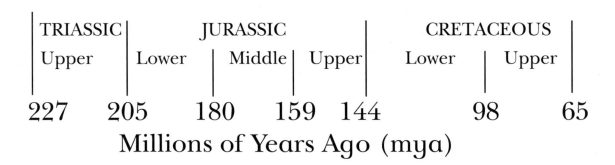

TRIASSIC		JURASSIC			CRETACEOUS	
Upper	Lower	Middle	Upper		Lower	Upper
227	205	180	159	144	98	65

Millions of Years Ago (mya)